HAL•LEONARD
VIOLIN
PLAY-ALONG

HOEDOWN

Jerry Loughney, violin
Jon Peik, guitar, mandolin, banjo, bass
Produced and Recorded by Dan Maske

ISBN 978-1-4768-1305-9

HAL•LEONARD®
CORPORATION
7777 W. BLUEMOUND RD. P.O. BOX 13819 MILWAUKEE, WI 53213

In Australia Contact:
Hal Leonard Australia Pty. Ltd.
4 Lentara Court
Cheltenham, Victoria, 3192 Australia
Email: ausadmin@halleonard.com.au

Visit Hal Leonard Online at
www.halleonard.com

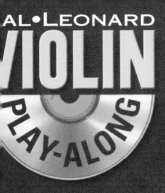

HAL•LEONARD
VIOLIN
PLAY-ALONG

HOEDOWN

CONTENTS

Arkansas Traveler

Southern American Folksong

(end manolin break)

Chicken Reel

By Joseph M. Daly

Optional: fiddle may *chop* or rest.

(end manolin break)

Cluck Old Hen

Traditional

banjo break

Optional: fiddle may *chop* or rest.

(end banjo break)

Cotton Eyed Joe

Tennessee Folksong

Optional: fiddle may *chop* or rest.

Girl I Left Behind Me

Traditional Irish

Over the Waterfall

Traditional

(end mandolin break)

The Red Haired Boy

Old Time Fiddle Tune

Turkey in the Straw

American Folksong

The Violin Play-Along Series

Play your favorite songs quickly and easily!

Just follow the music, listen to the CD to hear how the violin should sound, and then play along using the separate backing tracks. For PC and Mac computer users, the CD is enhanced so you can adjust the recording to any tempo without changing pitch!

1. Bluegrass
Foggy Mountain Breakdown • Gold Rush • John Hardy Was a Desperate Little Man • Orange Blossom Special • Panhandle Rag • Salty Dog Blues • Tennessee Waltz • You Don't Know My Mind.
00842152 Book/CD Pack $14.99

2. Popular Songs
Classical Gas • Come on Eileen • The Devil Went down to Georgia • Eleanor Rigby • Hurricane • Point of Know Return • Tradition.
00842153 Book/CD Pack $14.99

3. Classical
Canon in D (Pachelbel) • Concerto No. 1 in A Minor, Movement 1 (Bach) • Eine Kleine Nachtmusik (Serenade), First Movement (Mozart) • The Flight of the Bumble Bee (Rimsky-Korsakov) • Hungarian Dance No. 5 (Brahms) • Meditation (Massenet) • Romance in F (Beethoven) • Spring, First Movement (Vivaldi).
00842154 Book/CD Pack $14.99

4. Celtic
The Earl's Chair • Flowers of Edinburgh • The Gold Ring • Harvest Home • Haste to the Wedding • Julia Delaney • Lord Mayo (Tiarna Mhaigheo) • Rights of Man.
00842155 Book/CD Pack $14.99

5. Christmas Carols
Angels We Have Heard on High • Away in a Manger • Deck the Hall • The First Noel • Go, Tell It on the Mountain • Jingle Bells • Joy to the World • O Little Town of Bethlehem.
00842156 Book/CD Pack $14.99

6. Holiday Hits
Frosty the Snow Man • Here Comes Santa Claus (Right down Santa Claus Lane) • (There's No Place Like) Home for the Holidays • Jingle-Bell Rock • Let It Snow! Let It Snow! Let It Snow! • Merry Christmas, Darling • Rudolph the Red-Nosed Reindeer • Silver Bells.
00842157 Book/CD Pack $14.99

7. Jazz
Ain't Misbehavin' • Honeysuckle Rose • Limehouse Blues • Makin' Whoopee! • Ol' Man River • Pick Yourself Up • Speak Low • Tangerine.
00842196 Book/CD Pack $14.99

8. Country Classics
Crazy Arms • Faded Love • Heartaches by the Number • I'm Movin' On • Jambalaya (On the Bayou) • Louisiana Man • Tennessee River • Your Cheatin' Heart.
00842230 Book/CD Pack $12.99

9. Country Hits
Boot Scootin' Boogie • Born to Fly • Chattahoochee • Friends in Low Places • Guitars, Cadillacs • What Hurts the Most • Whose Bed Have Your Boots Been Under? • Wide Open Spaces.
00842231 Book/CD Pack $14.99

10. Bluegrass Favorites
Blue Moon of Kentucky • Blue Ridge Cabin Home • Blue Yodel No. 4 (California Blues) • Doin' My Time • I Am a Man of Constant Sorrow • Keep on the Sunny Side • Rocky Top • Uncle Pen.
00842232 Book/CD Pack $14.99

11. Bluegrass Classics
Bill Cheatham • Blackberry Blossom • Cripple Creek • Great Speckled Bird • Mule Skinner Blues • Red Wing • Roll in My Sweet Baby's Arms • Turkey in the Straw.
00842233 Book/CD Pack $14.99

12. Wedding Classics
Air on the G String • Ave Maria • Bridal Chorus • Canon in D • Jesu, Joy of Man's Desiring • Ode to Joy • Trumpet Voluntary • Wedding March.
00842324 Book/CD Pack $14.99

13. Wedding Favorites
All I Ask of You • In My Life • One Hand, One Heart • Somewhere Out There • Sunrise, Sunset • A Time for Us (Love Theme) • We've Only Just Begun • Wedding Processional.
00842325 Book/CD Pack $14.99

14. Blues Classics
Boom Boom • Born Under a Bad Sign • Dust My Broom • Hide Away • I'm Your Hoochie Coochie Man • Killing Floor • My Babe • Rock Me Baby.
00842427 Book/CD Pack $14.99

15. Stephane Grappelli
Django • It Don't Mean a Thing (If It Ain't Got That Swing) • Limehouse Blues • Minor Swing • Nuages • Ol' Man River • Stardust • The Way You Look Tonight.
00842428 Book/CD Pack $14.99

16. Folk Songs
Home on the Range • House of the Rising Sun • I've Been Working on the Railroad • Midnight Special • Nobody Knows the Trouble I've Seen • Scarborough Fair • When the Saints Go Marching In • Will the Circle Be Unbroken.
00842429 Book/CD Pack $14.99

17. Christmas Favorites
Blue Christmas • The Christmas Song (Chestnuts Roasting on an Open Fire) • Christmas Time Is Here • Do You Hear What I Hear • A Holly Jolly Christmas • I'll Be Home for Christmas • The Most Wonderful Time of the Year • White Christmas.
00842478 Book/CD Pack $14.99

18. Fiddle Hymns
Blessed Assurance • Down at the Cross (Glory to His Name) • He Keeps Me Singing • His Eye Is on the Sparrow • In the Garden • The Old Rugged Cross • Since Jesus Came into My Heart • Turn Your Eyes upon Jesus • Wayfaring Stranger • Wonderful Grace of Jesus.
00842499 Book/CD Pack $14.99

19. Lennon & McCartney
All My Loving • And I Love Her • A Day in the Life • Eleanor Rigby • I Saw Her Standing There • In My Life • Michelle • Yellow Submarine.
00842564 Book/CD Pack $14.99

20. Irish Tunes
The Irish Washerwoman • The Kesh Jig • King of the Fairies • The Little Beggarman • Mason's Apron • St. Anne's Reel • Star of Munster • Temperence Reel.
00842565 Book/CD Pack $14.99

21. Andrew Lloyd Webber
All I Ask of You • Any Dream Will Do • Don't Cry for Me Argentina • Memory • The Music of the Night • The Phantom of the Opera • Unexpected Song • Whistle Down the Wind.
00842566 Book/CD Pack $14.99

22. Broadway Hits
Castle on a Cloud • Dancing Queen • Defying Gravity • Fiddler on the Roof • I Whistle a Happy Tune • My Favorite Things • On My Own • Put On a Happy Face.
00842567 Book/CD Pack $14.99

23. Pirates of the Caribbean
Angelica • The Black Pearl • Davy Jones • Guilty of Being Innocent of Being Jack Sparrow • He's a Pirate • Jack Sparrow • The Medallion Calls • Two Hornpipes (Fisher's Hornpipe).
00842625 Book/CD Pack $14.99

24. Rock Classics
Baba O'Riley • Cherry Bomb • Dust in the Wind • Evil Woman • I Am the Walrus • Nights in White Satin • One More Cup of Coffee (Valley Below) • Sunday Bloody Sunday.
00842640 Book/CD Pack $14.99

25. Classical Masterpieces
Humoresque • Hungarian Dance No.2 (Brahms) • Rondo in D Major, K 485.
00842642 Book/CD Pack $14.99

26. Elementary Classics
Lied (Brahms) • Air (Finger) • Frölicher Tanz (Gluck) • Bourée (Handel) • Deutscher Tanz (Haydn) • Menuet (Lully) • Gavotte (Martini) • Andantino (Mozart) • Air (Purcell) • Ecossaise (Schubert) • March (Schumann) • Menuet (Telemann) • J'ai du bon tabac (traditional) • Waltz (von Weber).
00842643 Book/CD Pack $14.99

27. Classical Favorites
Bist Du Bei Mir • Eine Kleine Nachtmusik • He Shall Feed His Flock • Jesu, Joy of Man's Desiring • La Rejouissance • Minuet and Trio • Morning • Norwegian Dance.
00842646 Book/CD Pack $14.99

28. Classical Treasures
Air on the G String • Anitra's Dance • Arioso • Ave Maria • Elegy • Hornpipe • Largo • Last Spring • March • Minuetto • A Musical Joke • Sarabande.
00842647 Book/CD Pack $14.99

32. Favorite Christmas Songs
Believe • Have Yourself a Merry Little Christmas • It's Beginning to Look like Christmas • Let It Snow! Let It Snow! Let It Snow! • Sleigh Ride • Somewhere in My Memory • Walking in the Air • Winter Wonderland.
00102110 Book/CD Pack $14.99

www.halleonard.com

7777 W. Bluemound Rd. P.O. Box 13819 Milwaukee, WI 53213

Prices, contents, and availability subject to change without notice.

0612

The Violin Play-Along Series will help you play your favorite songs quickly and easily.
Just follow the music, listen to the CD to hear how the violin should sound, and then play
along using the separate backing tracks.

The CD is playable on any CD player, and is also enhanced so MAC and PC users can
adjust the recording to any tempo without changing the pitch.

Arkansas Traveler

Chicken Reel

Cluck Old Hen

Cotton Eyed Joe

Girl I Left Behind Me

Over the Waterfall

The Red Haired Boy

Turkey in the Straw

Book $6.99, CD $8.00 = **Pkg U.S. $14.99**
Parts not sold separately

HL00102161

HAL•LEONARD®

ISBN 978-1-4768-1305-9

Michael Daugherty

Raise the Roof
(for Timpani and Orchestra)

Solo Timpani Part

HENDON MUSIC

BOOSEY & HAWKES

DISTRIBUTED BY

HAL•LEONARD®